Popular PERFORMER

1950s

Arranged by LARRY SHACKLEY

The Best Songs from Broadway, Movies and Radio of the 1950s

The 1950s has left us with a stunning array of memorable and moving music. This volume revisits those songs, casting them in the rich voice of the piano. Popular songs that originated in Broadway musicals are represented such as "I Love Paris" from *Can-Can* (1953) and "I Could Have Danced All Night" from *My Fair Lady* (1956). There are also songs from the silver screen such as "When I Fall In Love" from *One Minute to Zero* (1952) and "The Man That Got Away," Judy Garland's famous number in *A Star is Born* (1954). The slinky melody of "Cry Me a River," the dancing syncopations of "Come Fly with Me," and all the other wonderful musical moments are certain to provide hours of enjoyment for the pianist who wishes to be a *Popular Performer*.

CONTENTS

ISBN-10: 0-7390-4502-4
ISBN-13: 978-0-7390-4502-2

A Day in the Life of a Fool
(Manha de Carnaval)

Music by Luiz Bonfá
English Lyric by Carl Sigman
Arr. Larry Shackley

Come Fly with Me

Lyric by Sammy Cahn
Music by James Van Heusen
Arr. Larry Shackley

CRY ME A RIVER

Words and Music by Arthur Hamilton
Arr. Larry Shackley

I Could Have Danced All Night

Lyrics by Alan Jay Lerner
Music by Frederick Loewe
Arr. Larry Shackley

I Love Paris

Words and Music by Cole Porter
Arr. Larry Shackley

The Man That Got Away

Words by Ira Gershwin
Music by Harold Arlen
Arr. Larry Shackley

Misty

Words by Johnny Burke
Music by Erroll Garner
Arr. Larry Shackley

Satin Doll

Words and Music by Johnny Mercer,
Duke Ellington and Billy Strayhorn
Arr. Larry Shackley

Teach Me Tonight

Words and Music by
Sammy Cahn and Gene DePaul
Arr. Larry Shackley

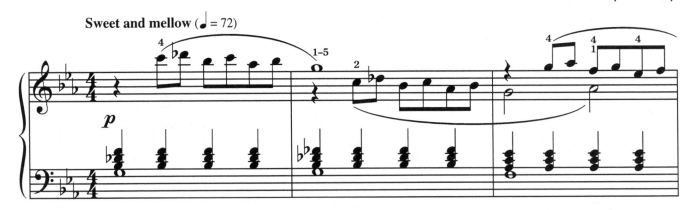

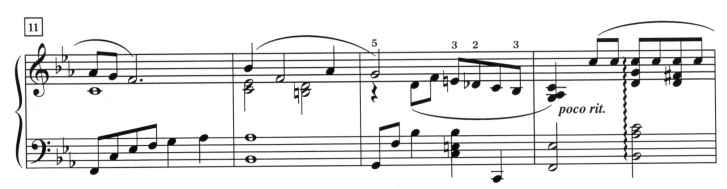

WHEN I FALL IN LOVE

Words by Edward Heyman
Music by Victor Young
Arr. Larry Shackley

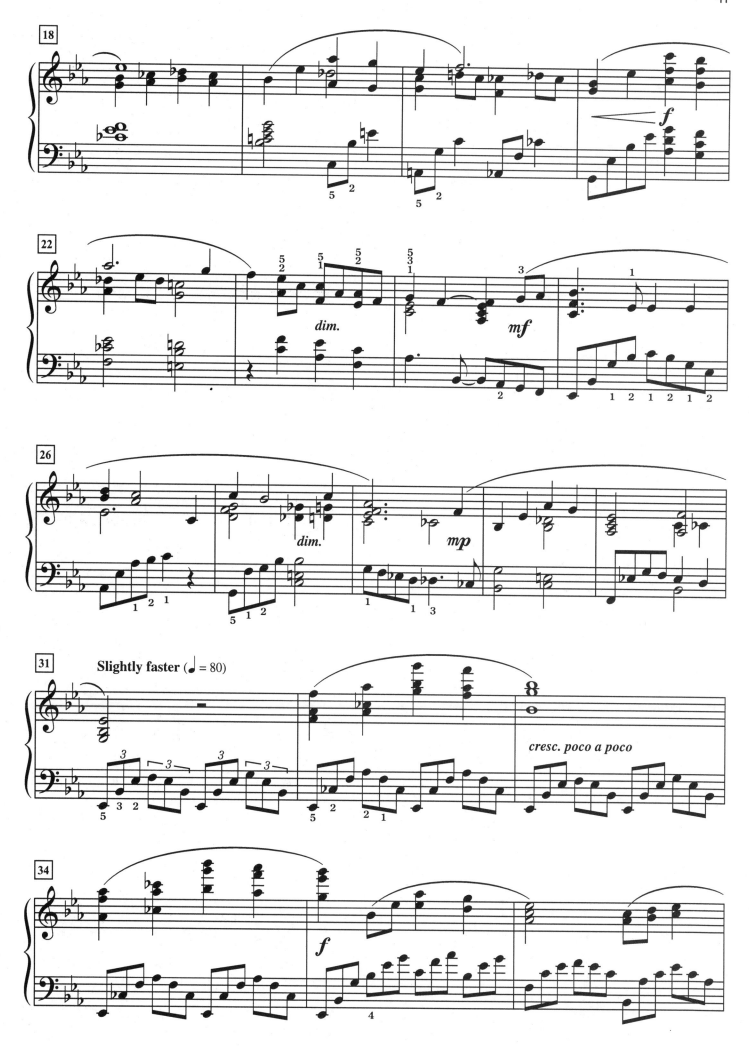

Hold Me, Thrill Me, Kiss Me

Words and Music by Harry Noble
Arr. Larry Shackley

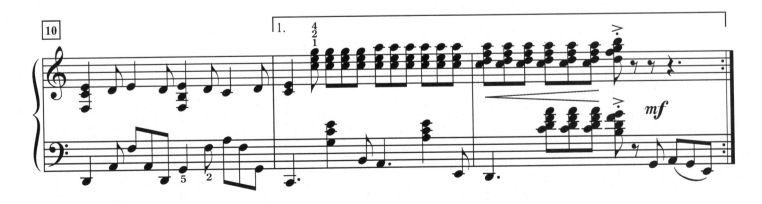